Taking appraisals & interviews

Taking appraisals & interviews

●●●●●■●●

JEAN CIVIL

WARD LOCK

To Barbara

A WARD LOCK BOOK

First published in the UK 1997
by Ward Lock
Wellington House
125 Strand
London
WC2 0BB

A Cassell Imprint

Distributed in the United States
by Sterling Publishing Co., Inc.
38 Park Avenue South, New York, NY 10016-8810

A British Library Cataloguing in Publication Data block for this book may be
obtained from the British Library

ISBN 0 7063 7704 4

Designed, edited and produced by Pardoe Blacker Publishing Ltd,
Lingfield, Surrey RH7 6BL

Printed in Hong Kong by Midas Printing Limited

CONTENTS

■ Introduction   9

■ Chapter 1: How do I relate to my staff?   13

   HOW GOOD A PEOPLE MANAGER AM I?   13

   QUESTIONNAIRE 1   13

   ANALYSIS OF QUESTIONNAIRE 1   15

   LEARN HOW TO MANAGE   23

   HOW GOOD ARE MY INTERVIEWING SKILLS?   25

   QUESTIONNAIRE 2   25

   WHAT SKILLS DO I NEED TO INTERVIEW   26
   MY STAFF EFFECTIVELY?

   INTERVIEWS ARE A TWO-WAY PROCESS   28

■ Chapter 2: Will my body language affect the person
             I am interviewing?   29

   QUESTIONNAIRE 3   30

   BODY LANGUAGE   32

   HOW CAN I CREATE RAPPORT?   51

   SUMMARY   55

■ Chapter 3: Six thoughts when interviewing 57

1. WILL THE SETTING AFFECT THE INTERVIEW PROCESS? 57

2. REMEMBER TO USE THE THREE-MINUTE RULE 63

3. DEALING WITH NEGATIVE PEOPLE

4. ENSURE THAT PEOPLE UNDERSTAND AND REMEMBER 68
WHAT YOU ARE TRYING TO SAY TO THEM

5. TRANSACTIONAL ANALYSIS 75

6. SOMETIMES I FIND IT DIFFICULT TO RELATE TO 76
SOME STAFF, WHEN INTERVIEWING OR TALKING
TO THEM

20 WAYS TO RELATE TO YOUR STAFF 77
MORE EFFECTIVELY

QUESTIONNAIRE 4 79

■ Chapter 4: How can I appraise staff effectively to get the best out of them? 81

QUESTIONNAIRE 5 83

HOW TO MANAGE OR IMPLEMENT AN 86
APPRAISAL SCHEME

PREPARATION FOR THE INTERVIEW 89

THE APPRAISAL INTERVIEW 91

HOW CAN I QUESTION STAFF WITHOUT THEM 92
FEELING THREATENED OR PATRONIZED?

USEFUL QUESTIONS TO ASK IN INTERVIEWS 95

THE BEGINNING OF THE INTERVIEW 95

THE MIDDLE OF THE INTERVIEW 96

LOOKING AT THE APPRAISEE'S NEEDS AND DEVELOPMENT	97
DEALING WITH DIFFICULT ISSUES	98
SETTING TARGETS	99
THE END OF THE INTERVIEW	100
HINTS ON HOW TO SET TARGETS	101
RECORDING TARGETS	103
THE A–Z OF GETTING THE BEST OUT OF YOUR STAFF	108

■ Conclusion

109

Acknowledgments

I would like to thank all the hundreds of managers I have met over the years as a Management Trainer, for their quotes, insights and stories. Hearing your stories made it possible for me to know and write about managers.

A special thank you to Jeannie Turnock for her computer skills in typing this book, and particularly for her excited interest and constant encouragement while I was writing it.

I am indebted to Norman Dickie, my co-trainer, for the witty – even rude – comments he made when he read the first drafts. He really helped me to focus.

I would also like to thank some great trainers with whom I have worked, Derek Marsh, Brenda Mallon, Colin Turner, Pablo Foster, Diane Brace and the late Bill Pasquerella, for their expertise, insights and humour on our training ventures.

Thanks go particularly to Mike Bryan, Ray Masters and the staff at Network Training. Then there are all the managers who have managed ME! In particular two terrific ones: Alan Chitty and Liz Balinger.

I am so grateful to my agent Alan Gordon Walker, who gave me confidence and made it all happen, and the superb staff at Pardoe Blacker.

Finally, but really by no means least, to my son Carl who did some word processing and commented on the contents, and my husband Geoff, who supported me emotionally and physically throughout the months of continuous work involved.

INTRODUCTION

The skills of interviewing and appraising are absolutely essential if you are going to get the best out of your staff. Being able to motivate, criticize, understand and praise at the right time will undoubtedly mean that you can help your staff and yourself to perform and so encourage an harmonious environment in which to work. But how can you do this? What specific skills do you require? This workbook highlights the the techniques you need within the context of your own management style, so you become aware of the attitudes and behaviour that affect the way you conduct interviews and appraisals.

A key objective in any appraisal is the assessment and creation of motivation in your staff as a demoralization leads to inefficiency in the workplace. A sign of demotivation is illness and absence. Perhaps some of your staff are absent through sickness more than others? Maybe you can identify certain individuals who, if there is a bug or virus going around the office will definitely pick it up.

This kind of problem which, if not addressed, could sap not only your energy, but also the energies of those around you, including the already demoralized staff member. For your own peace of mind, and that of your fellow sufferers, it is important that you recognize the problem and learn how to build upon the skills you already possess, in order to deal with it.

One way to encourage a spirit of enthusiasm is with praise.

A word of encouragement and appreciation when a job is done well is better than a tonic for the recipient. So when conducting your appraisals, remember that you will get much more out of you staff by congratulating them than by criticizing them.

This does not mean that you cannot criticize, but too many managers only criticize and forget the great human need to feel valued or prized by their manager. Of course there are managers who believe that, if they are liked, they are not managing properly, so they exhibit and communicate a lack of care and concern for the people who work with them.

You may be lucky and have motivated staff about you, either because you manage in a way that creates motivated people or because they are naturally good at motivating themselves. However, a demotivated and discouraged staff could also develop because of your style or because there are demoralizing problems at work. This book will help you assess your style so that you can make the changes necessary to perform well with your staff.

The interview and the appraisal are ideal opportunities for both parties to discuss problems and aspirations. Both people can put forward their points of view. When conducted successfully this usually results in a greater understanding on both sides.

Formal appraisals are meetings that help to keep a check on progress and are normally held at least annually. They are sometimes linked to pay and conditions and so frequent one-to-one meetings allow for on-going reviews and the handling of day-to-day matters as they arise.

Interviews, on the other hand, are mostly used when taking on new staff and in reviewing performance, which may be a stressful situation linked to problems at work. They are also used to discuss salaries and conditions. Managers who possess effective interviewing skills will find they have an invaluable asset in their job because these skills can be used in so many situations.

It is for this reason that this particular workbook concentrates on the art of interviewing in different contexts as well as on appraising and motivating your staff.

Each of the chapters has a questionnaire to enable you to focus and reflect on your particular management approach. Where it is applicable, models are given to widen your knowledge or understanding. Also, most of the chapters contain a checklist as a quick guide to your being able to get the best out of your staff.

The book begins, therefore, with a questionnaire in order to raise your awareness of aspects of your 'people management' style; this is followed by a section looking at the common or core skills, and at specific skills required when interviewing people for differing purposes and in different types of interview. All interviews are two-way and both interviewer and interviewee need to understand certain skills. For you, as a manager, will no doubt have to undergo interviews, as well as being an interviewer yourself. These core skills include how to create rapport, how your body 'speaks', how to actively listen and reflect, and how to use succinct language and questions in a way that gives you your desired outcome, enabling you to empathize, reframe, and to give and receive feedback.

Some managers will find the idea of interviews being a two-way process difficult because of their personality, lack of skills, different belief and value systems, or fear of intimacy. Others may feel fine and will enjoy relating to their staff.

Of course, there are not just these two scenarios. It is more likely that you will have some days when you want to be involved and others when you resist. But, as a manager, you will have to exhibit your relating skills regardless of how you feel. This is a necessary part of your job, even though it is difficult when you are having a bad day and do not particularly share the values of the person you are relating to. However, you can make it easier for yourself by learning the art of interviewing as a skill to be used as you need it.

After covering interviewing skills, you can move on to the specific skills needed in appraisals. This involves considering the implication of an appraisal system, the core skills of appraising staff and giving training in appraisal skills, and in addressing difficult situations. The importance of questioning is addressed in detail and guidance is also given on the setting of targets.

Finally, there is a chapter on how to motivate, value and praise your staff. This looks at varied research that has been undertaken on the subject of motivation. You are then asked to consider the importance of praising your staff, both as a motivator and as a way of getting the best out of your staff. This chapter concludes with a questionnaire enabling you to assess if you are a motivating manager.

Begin with the first questionnaire, remembering that with all such questionnaires there is a Health Warning: there are no right or wrong answers, but do be honest and avoid responding with 'It depends'. I know it depends. However, the purpose is to raise your awareness and to help you recognize your behaviour or attitudes in given settings. The questionnaires are incorporated to assist and encourage you, not to demoralize you or catch you out. Celebrate your successful skills and discover those on which you need to work.

Now turn to Questionnaire 1, then check your score against the analysis. See how you fare.

CHAPTER

How do I relate to my staff?

How good a people manager am I?

QUESTIONNAIRE 1
● ●

The following questions are designed to encourage you to
take a fresh look at your management systems, day-to-day
operations, personnel skills, personal style and appraisal ability. Answer honestly yes or no to the following 20 questions.
Avoid answering 'It depends', 'Maybe' or 'Sometimes' as
these answers usually mean 'No'.

		Yes	No
1	Are my job interviews based on an unbiased selection policy?	☐	☐
2	Am I relaxed and confident about interviewing staff?	☐	☐
3	Have I established a staff mentoring system?		
4	Are all my staff working to their full potential?	☐	☐

5   Do I encourage my staff to bring
    ideas to me?   ☐   ☐
6   Do I hold open meetings where staff
    can suggest agenda items?   ☐   ☐
7   Am I able to deal with my staff's
    personal issues and concerns?   ☐   ☐
8   Do I genuinely praise staff face-to-face
    when they have been successful?   ☐   ☐
9   Do I know how to motivate individual
    members of my staff?   ☐   ☐
10 Am I able to resolve conflict?   ☐   ☐
11 Am I able to negotiate when there
    are differing needs?   ☐   ☐
12 Am I able to manage 'marginal performers'?   ☐   ☐
13 Do I formally appraise staff annually?   ☐   ☐
14 Do I set targets jointly with my staff?   ☐   ☐
15 Do I give regular monthly formal
    or informal feedback?   ☐   ☐
16 When I delegate, do I give all relevant
    information and also delegate the
    power and support that goes with the job?   ☐   ☐
17 Do I socialize with my staff?   ☐   ☐
18 Do I know how I am perceived by my staff?   ☐   ☐
19 Do I respond to staff training needs?   ☐   ☐
20 Do I have a weekly open-door policy?   ☐   ☐

SCORE SHEET

Put a 1 for a Yes, and a 0 for a No against the question numbers in the following five columns (Table 1). This will give you separate scores for each of the five management aspects. Then add all your scores together to get your TOTAL SCORE.

TABLE 1

	Mgt systems (SY)	Mgt day-to-day (D)	Mgt skills (SK)	Mgt style (ST)	Mgt sppraisal (A)
	1	4	2	11	13
	3	5	7	12	14
	6	8	10	16	18
	20	9	15	17	19
Total					
				Grand total	

How did you do?

18-20   Well done, an excellent performance!

10-17   You are getting the best out of most of your staff.

3-9   You need to improve your management skills.

0-2   Hopefully, this book will provide you with help in this important area.

Analysis of Questionnaire 1

If you really want to get the best out of your staff, let us take a look at what you need to do. Each of the twenty questions is now addressed. These indicate different aspects of your management role and are initialled to indicate the following: SY: systems; D: day-to-day; SK: skills; ST: style and A: appraisal. Pay particular attention to those questions in which you scored a 'No'.

Question 1: Have an unbiased selection policy (SY)

It is vitally important that job interviews are based on a 'fair selection' policy and that you recognize legal and equal opportunity policies, not only in your interviews but also in your publicity. You are not going to be able to get the best out of your staff if you give out messages that you are biased or prejudiced. Make it clear you offer opportunities regardless of race, gender, disability, sexual orientation or age.

Question 2: Enjoying interviewing your staff (SK)

It will give you a strong edge as a manager if you are able to be relaxed and confident when interviewing your staff. More importantly, you are more likely to achieve your desired outcomes if you are relaxed. The interviewee will pick up the signals and therefore be able to be much more open and honest with you. Conversely, your tension and anxiety can seep through, contaminating and affecting the reactions of the interviewee.

Question 3: Accept that staff need support (SY)

When new staff join your organization it is essential to have a mentoring system so that they can ask questions about their work and company systems. The mentor can be the line manager or a colleague, depending on the size of your organization. Having a staff mentoring system is not necessarily only for new staff joining an organization. It is also a very useful tool with which to encourage staff development within the organization. 'Learning by sitting next to Nelly' or 'shadowing', where a member of staff works alongside an expert in his or her particular sphere in order to learn their role, skills, or job, can be particularly useful for potential managers. Such training enables them to gain a fuller and more holistic understanding of the work involved within their organization. It can also be supportive of staff and create a greater understanding of different roles within the organization.

Question 4: Address the situation if staff are not working to their full potential (D)

When staff are not working to their full potential, the situation should be addressed. You need to sit down with them, interview them, and establish what may be the reasons. If they have personal concerns, you will need to support them. On the other hand, if the cause is because they 'can't' or 'won't' then you will have to give them feedback about their performance. Try to establish whether they feel they are not being stretched in their job and need new challenges.

Question 5: Truly ask for ideas and suggestions (D)

Many staff may feel reluctant to bring ideas to you for the simple reason that they do not want to look stupid, feel embarrassed or be rejected. If you want to improve that situation genuinely, let them know that you welcome ideas. Explain that not always will these ideas be acted upon, but you would hope that out of every ten ideas there will be at least one good one, even though the other nine may not be practical or viable. If that is your attitude then people will want to be involved with you and will go along with you and support you as a manager. Encouraging your staff brings you greater rewards.

Question 6: Vary your meetings (SY)

In order to get the best out of a meeting, you need at some point to have open agendas to empower the staff to bring forward aspects of their work which they would like to have included or discussed. While formal meetings are important, making them relevant to the people present also enables you to get more out of your staff. When your employees feel that there is some commitment on management's behalf, and they are being listened to, morale is raised. When employees' views are considered seriously and ideas are acted upon, this helps to build their self-esteem, self-image and their positive involvement with the work-place and its management.

Question 7: Counsel and support your staff (SK)

Virtually all staff at some point are trying to deal with personal issues and concerns to a greater or lesser degree. Some of your staff may be directly affected by what is happening to them at home. This may become apparent by a change in their behaviour, work patterns, relationships or lower output. Others may, in fact, respond by becoming workaholics and resorting to frantic activity as their coping mechanism. Whichever way they respond, it is important for you to be skilful enough to be able to deal with their personal issues and concerns. We will look into this in greater detail later in the book.

Question 8: Praise, praise, praise (D)

There is no praise like that of a manager's praise, which you will be giving day-to-day, throughout the year, but you also need to be skilled at praising in the appraisal situation. You will have external pressures and deadlines to meet, but relating genuinely to people is essential. It is vital to have face-to-face conversations, particularly to learn about your staff and to know how to give real praise in a way that builds up and encourages your staff. If you experienced lots of praise as a child, you are likely to do this more easily and openly. If, however, you were brought up in a critical environment, you may find that you are behaving in the same way to others. If you are a parent, sometimes you will recognize yourself saying the same things that were said to you (even things you hated hearing at the time) and you will just go on re-scripting. Planning is an important management skill and you will need to be able to say 'Thank you, I really appreciate that' or 'I thought you did that job really well'. Remember, staff will grow with praise and shrivel with criticism.

Question 9: Motivate your staff (D)

Knowing how to motivate your staff, recognizing what 'different strokes for different folks' are needed, is one of the key skills you, as a manager, need to acquire. If you find it difficult to do this, you need to concentrate on this area. Some managers find it hard to say 'Well done', but without this you will not be developing your staff's unused potential and definitely not getting the best out of them.

Question 10: Handle any conflict (SK)

Some managers won't handle conflict because they believe that by avoiding it they will save upsetting people's feelings, but if you avoid conflict you will exacerbate situations. Do you avoid, or are you aggressive? Do you want people to like you so much that you pull back and merely smile in order to appease? Or are you more like a chameleon, changing your colours according to the environment, and finding that you compromise so that no one feels totally successful? An effective manager gets the best out of his or her staff and it is vital that you acquire the skills of addressing conflict directly, thereby working towards a win-win situation. You need to be able to say what you are observing, how you are feeling and what you actually need from your staff. If you can do this consistently, you will gain a far greater insight into your own needs and achieve a greater empathy with how your staff may be feeling.

Question 11: Swap ideas to achieve win-win (ST)

Negotiation takes a great deal of skill, and it is a wise manager who recognizes that sometimes management and staff may have different requirements. This needs to be talked through and your staff need to realize what is expected of them. By making this clear, you are highly likely to succeed. Half the time you may be expecting your staff to be able to read your mind, or just to do what they have been told. Some of your staff need explanations. Once they know your reasoning, they are more likely to feel inclined to go along with you.

Question 12: Have early discussions with under-performing staff (ST)

Managing staff who are not performing as well as you expect them to, requires action, both for your own sake and that of your other staff. The problem needs to be addressed. By doing this in the early stages, you will avoid all kinds of disciplinary or competence issues at a later stage.

Question 13: Appraise or review your staff (A)

Appraisal is a wonderful opportunity for staff to have your undivided attention. Done well, an appraisal system will motivate staff and can be used as a jumping-off point to improve staff development. This is looked at in detail in a later chapter.

Question 14: Jointly set realistic targets (A)

One of the known causes of stress is not being able to achieve targets set by a manager, so when setting targets it is important to allow staff to set their own targets first, before you add yours. In this way, the member of staff will feel more committed to meeting your aims than if you use authoritarian or dictatorial methods of imposing targets. Do it jointly and staff will be far more motivated to achieve those targets.

Question 15: Ask staff how they are doing (SK)

When did you last speak to your staff, simply to say 'How are you doing?' Are you so busy yourself that you are forgetting that they would appreciate the opportunity to express their interest in their work, and also in your work. They need regular feedback about how you evaluate their work. Equally, you

can ask them how you are doing. It cannot be emphasized suffi-
ciently that human contact, a smile and a 'how are you today?'
will motivate staff far better than pages of impersonal memos.

Question 16: Delegate with power (ST)

Some managers find it very hard to delegate because they are
either concerned that the person may do better than they
can, or they are in such a hurry themselves that they think that
by the time they have explained the procedure to someone else,
they could have done the task themselves. It is important that
when you delegate a task, you also delegate the power that
goes with the job, otherwise you will leave staff feeling inse-
cure and often unable to make decisions. They need to be
reassured that whatever decisions they make, you will back
them. Also, they need to be given all the information relating
to that delegation.

Question 17: Occasionally socialize with staff (ST)

You may have a management style in which you like to socialize with your staff. Socializing with staff can be very positive,
but some managers may, however unwittingly, use this as a
way of pressurizing their staff. Socializing is one thing and it is
often welcomed, although you must recognize that sometimes
staff do not want you to be present at certain gatherings.
They may want to discuss your present 'flavour of the month'
or your positive or unreasonable attitude or behaviour
towards them. You need to be aware of the fine balance
between your presence or absence being acceptable.

A word of warning: if you socialize to an extent that is
perceived as harassment, or certainly, if you become emotionally or sexually involved with any member of your staff, this
is highly likely to have great detrimental effect on how your
staff perceive you, and how they behave towards you. The

first time MANAGER

ramifications of a too-close relationship with a member of staff within your direct team can have disastrous consequences. However, having said that, many permanent partnerships began in the workplace.

Question 18: Ask your staff for feedback (A)

The perception of your staff could be very different from *your* ideas of how you are managing them. Getting and giving feedback is, therefore, essential. You could be thinking that you are a good manager, when in fact your staff think otherwise, so ask them. The staff need to know where they are at, what you think of them and how they are doing, but this should be a two-way process. If you are a manager who really wants to get the best out of people, then you will also be asking them for feedback about how you are doing. In what ways can you support them, monitor their workload, and enhance their career and aspirations? You have to be a superb manager to be confident enough to say 'How am I doing?', as well as recognizing the need to give feedback to others. This is particularly important in appraisals and one-to-one meetings throughout the year.

Question 19: Respond to their training needs (A)

Having appraised staff, you should be able to identify their staff training needs. This in itself is often difficult, but it can certainly demotivate staff if needs are identified but nothing follows. Although this is a major part of appraisal interviews, it also needs to be addressed in one-to-one meetings throughout the year. So in order to motivate and get the best out of your employees, try to arrange training that is applicable, desirable, informative and, most importantly, fun.

Question 20: Operate a timed open-door policy (SY)

Having an open-door policy is fine, but alongside that must be, for your own sanity, a closed-door policy to allow you to get on with things you need to do. However, if at least once a week staff feel that there is a time when you will make yourself available, when they could come and talk to you, that might help to get the best out of them.

Your availability is probably more important to people than you realize. Some staff emotionally perceive their managers as parents, and maybe experience sibling rivalry, wanting to be near them and gain their attention or approval. So, at least once a week, an open-door policy would seem an ideal for which to aim so that your staff will have access to you, to be near you and, therefore, may be able to gain your attention or approval. Try it out and see what happens.

Learn how to manage

How did you score in Questionnaire 1 when asked about your interviewing skills? Read on and perhaps you can find some new ways in which you can try to get the best out of your staff.

Some managers withdraw from 'people contact' and prefer to communicate through memos, e-mail or through others, rather than speak directly to the person concerned. But if you really want to improve your management techniques, thus improving staff morale and getting the best out of your workforce, then you will need to learn how to MANAGE:

M	Motivate
A	Appraise
N	Negotiate
A	Appreciate
G	Give feedback
E	Empower

first time MANAGER

All of these processes require you to be able to interview people in a way that encourages them to be open and honest. You will need to be proficient when interviewing them. This does not only apply to job or appraisal interviews, but to every time you have a meeting with a member of your staff.

One of the most difficult scenarios for you might be finding out how to motivate your staff.

Your appraisal skills may need refining. There will be times when you will need to negotiate so that both of you feel that you have gained something – that means working towards a win-win situation. On other occasions you may need to appreciate what your staff have been able to achieve and accomplish. You will be giving feedback regularly, to give positive guidance or to resolve difficulties that have arisen. Also, you will need to empower your staff on a regular basis to enable them to deal with work or personal issues, thus getting the best out of them.

All of these aspects of management involve you having to 'interview' or to meet with your staff. So let us begin by recognizing your present interviewing skills and strengths, and areas on which you may need to work.

Now turn to and answer Questionnaire 2.

How good are my interviewing skills?

QUESTIONNAIRE 2

● ●

A general questionnaire to raise awareness about your interviewing skills and past interviewing experiences.

Do you like interviewing people?　　　　　Yes ☐　No ☐

Give five words to describe
interviews for you.

_____

_____

_____

_____

Name different types of
interviews in which you
have been involved.

_____

_____

_____

What skills do you think
you need to interview
effectively?

_____

_____

_____

_____

In which of these skills are
you confident of your ability?

_____

_____

_____

_____

Have you ever appointed someone　　Yes ☐　No ☐
in whom you have been delighted?

Have you ever made an appointment　　Yes ☐　No ☐
in which you have been disappointed?

Analysis of this questionnaire will be addressed in the following discussions. If your five words are positive, then you are likely to be a skilled interviewer. If you have chosen some negative words, then help is at hand.

What skills do I need to interview my staff effectively?

There are different ways of managing people, different styles, approaches and philosophies, but one thing you will need to do well, whatever your management philosophy, is to relate to your staff. You can do this by interviewing effectively.

While there are many different types of interview with which you are already familiar and probably skilled, it is likely that you can develop your present skills even further.

Let us begin by considering and comparing the following different interviews:

Job interviews
Appraisal interviews
Counselling/helping interviews
Interviews where you have to manage conflict
Disciplinary interviews.

Although these interviews have different purposes and outcomes, they do share common skills. Also, there are some specific skills required in certain situations.

These are identified in Table 2:

TABLE 2 Shared and specific skills in differing interviews

SHARED SKILLS	TYPES OF INTERVIEW					
	Job	Appraise	Support counselling	Competence	Discipline	Conflict
Enabling body language	✓	✓	✓	✓	✓	✓
Creating rapport	✓	✓	✓	✓	✓	✓
Active listening	✓	✓	✓	✓	✓	✓
Reflecting	✓	✓	✓	✓	✓	✓
Asking open questions	✓	✓	✓	✓	✓	✓
Asking clarifying questions	✓	✓	✓	✓	✓	✓
Empathy	✓	✓	✓	✓	✓	✓
Checking out	✓	✓	✓	✓	✓	✓
Feeding back	✓	✓	✓	✓	✓	✓
Using succinct language	✓	✓	✓	✓	✓	✓
Reframing	✓	✓	✓	✓	✓	✓
Assertiveness skills	✓	✓	✓	✓	✓	✓
SPECIFIC SKILLS						
Asking closed questions	✓				✓	✓
Freeing skills		✓	✓	✓		
Praising staff		✓	✓	✓	✓	✓
Motivating staff		✓	✓	✓		✓
Honouring confidentiality	✓	✓	✓	✓	✓	
Setting targets		✓		✓		

Interviews are a two-way process

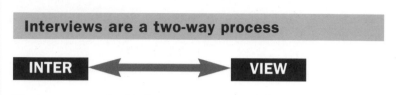

Having acquired all the interviewing skills you need, now think about the importance of making the interview a two-way process, as you will gain insight into how the other person thinks or feels and vice versa.

TYPE OF INTERVIEW	PERSON		ROLE
Any interview	Interviewee	⟷	Interviewer
Job interview	Candidate	⟷	Member(s) of panel
Appraisal	Appraisee	⟷	Appraiser
Counselling Helping	Client or colleague	⟷	Counsellor Manager
Competence interview	Under-performer	⟷	Manager
Managing conflict	Other person(s)	⟷	Self
Disciplinary interview	Staff member	⟷	Manager or tribunal member(s)

Finally, it is important to recognize that the language used, the roles, and reasons, for the interview may be different, but they still need to be a two-way process.

CHAPTER

Will my body language affect the person I am interviewing?

es. In terms of your body language, you are likely to be aware that certain body positions can trigger certain perceptions in other people's minds. Although you may not really think it matters, you are wrong – it does. It is not what you think you are sending, but what is actually being received. 'It's not what you say, it's the way that you say it.'

So test it out. Begin by looking at the following illustrations and write down what you would feel or think about a person if they were to use such a gesture.

Some managers may find this difficult and respond with 'Nothing – I'm not affected by body language. I don't stereotype people'. Well, good for you, but I believe you will be affected subconsciously, if not consciously, by how people use their bodies.

So many managers, with whom I have worked as a trainer, have initially laughed at the idea, only to be converted to its importance. Usually this happens because they have received feedback from other delegates on the same course about their negative perceptions of the cynic's body language.

Most certainly your staff will be affected by how your body talks to them, but they are unlikely to tell you, unless of course you have such a good relationship that you can ask for honest feedback. So before giving you some thoughts on how your body talks to people, turn to Questionnaire 3.

QUESTIONNAIRE 3

● ●

What messages are you picking up from the following gestures?

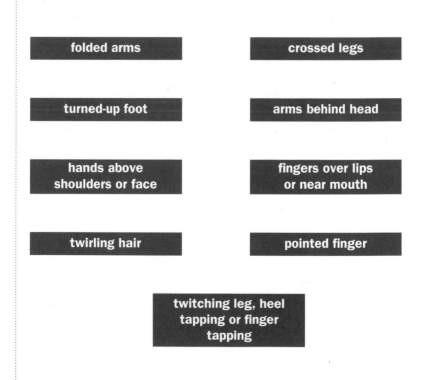

folded arms	crossed legs
turned-up foot	arms behind head
hands above shoulders or face	fingers over lips or near mouth
twirling hair	pointed finger
twitching leg, heel tapping or finger tapping	

■ Possible feelings or thoughts exhibited

TABLE 3

BODY TALK	NEGATIVE IMPRESSION TRANSMITTED
Folded arms	Uncomfortable: don't want to be here
Crossed legs	Keep your distance
Turned-up foot	Uncomfortable with what you are saying or what is being asked of you
Arms behind the head	'One day you'll be as intelligent as I am.' or Open and too relaxed to be taking the interview seriously
Hands above shoulders or face	De-powering
Fingers over lips or fingers near mouth	Censoring, concerned about what is being said
Twirling hair	Anxious, childish, nervous. Some think it is sexy
Pointed finger	Accusative, critical
Twitching leg, heel tapping or finger tapping	Stressed, wish to hurry, not really interested

It is important to give positive rather than negative messages to your staff if you want to get the best out of them. So let us now look in detail at how your body can talk.

Body language

Does my body language give me away?

Never underestimate your body language, for how you use your body almost certainly affects how your staff react to you. It is, however, an area that is often dismissed as psychological gobbledegook, or there is a reluctance to accept its relevance.

When someone talks to you, you are only hearing a small percentage of what they are actually saying, and you are picking up a greater percentage of information through the messages which are being given by their body. You may be doing this unconsciously, but nevertheless it is affecting how you are thinking or feeling about that person. For example, saying something positive to someone, but also pointing your finger, will be picked up as criticism rather than praise.

Begin reading the following section, suspending your disbelief and trying to ascertain if there might be something in it for you. Nobody likes to be told what they are doing is wrong, so I expect that you will agree with some of the following comments and disagree with others. The intention is simply to open your mind to new ideas. If you do not like them, then shut the doors, but remember there are consequences for each option we take in life and the consequence for you might be that your staff are picking up very different messages from your body language than you intend to convey. It's not what you think you are saying that is important but what is 'heard' or 'seen' by others.

Remember there are cultural differences in different parts of the world. Some of the gestures I refer to are multi-cultural, others may belong just to the western world. For example, in the western world, looking into people's eyes when they are talking to you creates the impression that you are listening, whereas in other cultures this may be seen as disrespectful. Similarly, people of different nationalities may have different personal spaces. Some people will naturally move very close to the person to whom they are speaking, whereas in other countries this may not be regarded as acceptable behaviour.

So how do different parts of the body talk to us?

Head talk

The nodding of the head almost universally indicates 'yes', or agreement, whereas the shaking of the head implies the opposite, that is, refusing or disagreeing.

When people are happy they smile: when they are miserable they frown or grimace.

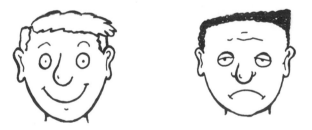

Facial expressions are particular give-aways: the raising of an eyebrow may indicate puzzlement.

The raising of the forehead might be amazement.

Eye talk

In neuro-linguistic terms it is thought that people will move their eyes in different directions depending on what they are doing, thinking or feeling. These pictures are mirror images of their eyes as you see them: as they raise their eyes to the left (to the right as you look at them) they are trying to recall incidents. . .

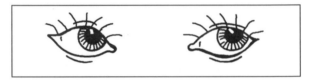

To the left, they are creating visually or constructing images.

Looking straight at you means they are listening and slightly to the right shows they are recalling and remembering what they or you have said.

However, when the eyes are lowered it means people are influenced by kinosthetics, emotions or feelings; lowered and slightly to the left indicates feelings; and to the right, talking to oneself.

Of course, some people could still be listening to you with their eyes lowered, because what is being said between you is creating a set of positive or negative emotions in them. Also, some people will close their eyes when they are trying to see something, or want to withhold their feelings.

The raising of the eyes to the left or to the right are reversed by 6 per cent of the population. Many of the people in this group are left-handed, but not all. So, in some instances, the eyes move in the opposite direction to that which has been described.

How to relate this information to your management skills when interviewing

If you ask someone, 'What have been your successes over the last year?', they are likely to *recall* the images visually. When you ask, 'Where do you see yourself in two years' time?' they are likely to *construct* the image visually. 'What did he say to you?' leads to *auditory recall*; 'What do you think you will say to her at your next meeting?' *auditory construct*; 'How do you feel about not getting your promotion?' *a kinosthetic response*, and 'What might you say to yourself before your next demonstration?' leads to an *auditory dialogue*.

Face talk

It is not only the movements of the face but also the movements of the hands on the face that indicate when somebody is lying or concerned whether to say anything or not:

The hand across the mouth and

the finger on the lip may perhaps
indicate not wanting to disclose something.

Lifting the hands above the shoulders and fiddling with hair can disempower you ...

Stroking a beard

or sucking your glasses

may again take away your power. The sucking of glasses is also supposed to indicate that you are waiting for time or 'thinking it over' time.

Shoulder talk

The shoulder shrug is usually accepted as meaning 'I don't quite understand: I don't really know what you are talking about', whereas if the shoulders are lifted, with tension around them, this may indicate fear. We lodge fear in our shoulders, anger in our calves and, supposedly, sexual problems in the lower back.

If your arms are folded, this can indicate that you want to block somebody out or, more likely, that you are feeling

uncomfortable with yourself or the situation you are in. Many people will say 'I only cross my arms like this because it makes me feel more comfortable', and they are right, because when we are feeling uncomfortable we give ourselves a little cuddle.

Touch talk

A lot of information can be gleaned from touch. The most likely tactile interaction in management is probably going to be the handshake. In terms of hands, you can have a submissive hand, where the palm is uppermost, or a dominant hand, where the palm is lowered. Shaking hands can create a tremendous impression on your first meeting with someone. If you are shaking hands, then do so with your hand as far up to the other person's thumb as you possibly can. Shake firmly, for there is nothing worse than a limp, wet-trout handshake.

Equally, it is just as offputting if you shake hands with a vice-like grip that almost cuts rings into your victim's fingers.

So give a positive handshake...

Statements like 'shake like a man' are often indicators of firm-ness and power.

Then there is the gloved handshake, where someone will put both their hands around yours, shaking with one hand and covering the back of your palm with the other. This may make people feel smothered or intimidated.

In some countries people may hold your elbow, wrist, upper arm or even your shoulder while shaking your hand.

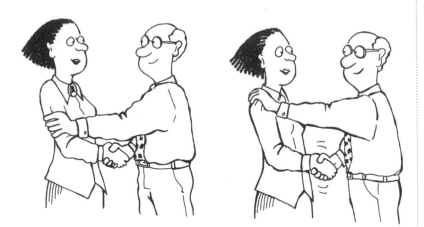

Hand talk

If somebody is sitting with their elbows on the table and their intertwined fingers, blocking their body, this indicates a tendency to hold in negative feelings, even though they may be smiling. Intertwined fingers indicate resistance, whereas open hands show acceptance.

The higher the hands are held, the more resistant the person is. However, clenched hands held low down the body would still tend to keep people at bay.

Then there is the 'steepling' of hands. The 'raised steeple' indicates a superior to a subordinate interaction, a kind of know-it-all or confident attitude. Managers often use this gesture when they want to give advice to their subordinates. (A dreadful word! However, many management books and managers use this word instead of 'colleagues' or 'staff'.)

This gesture is particularly common among lawyers and accountants. The 'lowered steeple' indicates that you are listening rather than feeling in control and superior.

Ear talk

The ear-rub may indicate that you really don't want to hear any more, or you have heard enough and would like to talk yourself.

Neck talk

The neck-scratch is supposed to indicate 'I don't know if that is correct, really'.

Then there is the collar-pull. The author and anthropologist, Desmond Morris found that when people were lying there was a tingling sensation around the face and neck tissues which needed to be rubbed or scratched to ease it. This may also be the case when somebody is angry or frustrated and needs to pull their collar away from their neck. Of course, it could just mean that they are hot, or that the collar is uncomfortable.

Leg talk

As well as crossing arms, many people cross their legs, which again pushes people away and can show that you are uncomfortable. Possibly you are feeling very comfortable, but again it is useful to realize that what is important is not what you think you are saying with your body, but what is being picked up by the messages you are sending out.

If someone crosses their arms and legs, they look as if they are going to be very difficult to convince, making it difficult for you to get across what you are trying to say to them. Alternatively this may indicate displeasure before or during the conversation.

Some people will cross their legs and hold on to the leg as a barrier, a kind of arm-lock or leg-lock. This position means that the person is rather stubborn or tough-minded, making it difficult to break through their present attitude.

Sit talk

How you sit as a manager will be giving all kinds of messages. Let us look at the following possibilities.

There are conflicting thoughts about some-one who sits with their arms behind their head.

Either that person comes across as 'one day you will be as intelligent as I am', or they look so laid-back that they don't appear to be taking very seriously what you may be saying to them.

Where you sit on the chair can indicate various things. If someone is leaning forward, then this is an invasion of the speaker's space. They look as if they are ready to finish talking to you.

If they are sitting with one arm hooked on the back of a chair, this may be giving the impression of 'I really don't want to be here'.

Very few people sit with their feet up on the desk but this would be about ownership and claiming their territory.

If someone is relaxed enough to sit with one leg over the arm of a chair, then they really are coming over as someone who has not got a great deal of concern for what you have to say.

Finger talk

Then there is the pointed finger. If you point your finger at people you must be being critical; you cannot say anything supportive and helpful if your finger is wagging. Some managers may know better than actually to point a finger, but instead they use a pen, or anything else that is likely to be dictatorial, in the message they are delivering.

Foot talk

Finally, the big give-away is the feet. If someone turns their foot up then this indicates that they are uncomfortable, either with the question you have just asked them or with what they are at present saying. This gesture is called 'crying with the feet' in the field of social work. In fact, so much knowledge can be gained by learning how to interpret the signals transmitted by people's feet, that everyone should have a special course on the subject.

To summarize: be aware that there may be many reasons for people moving their bodies in certain ways. A good rule

of thumb is to sit in an 'open' body position while keeping as still as you possibly can; this will make the other person feel more relaxed and comfortable in your presence. Recognize that your body talk may well be sending out negative messages that could be the exact opposite of what you intend to convey. If you think this applies to you, remember that the Golden Rule is to 'fake it till you make it'.

first time MANAGER

Fake it till you make it

Ten tips on how to use your body effectively in an interview

1	Shake hands firmly, not aggressively
2	Smile only when genuinely pleased
3	Keep arms below shoulders
4	Do not cross legs
5	Put feet firmly on the floor
6	Keep arms open
7	Keep hands relaxed
8	Have an open, accepting body posture
9	Keep still: stillness is empowering
10	Hold your head at the same angle as the interviewee

How can I create rapport?

Sixty to eighty per cent of human communication is non-verbal.

When you are managing people with whom you feel comfortable, you are likely to demonstrate this ease by your body language. Equally, any lack of ease will also be conveyed through your body language. Remember, though, that this is only one small facet of yourself, and be aware that you may be a good manager but with irritating mannerisms.

Now think about your gestures in different situations. When you are in a one-to-one discussion or in a meeting, are you giving off positive or negative signals? Many managers discount the idea that positive body language enhances their ability to manage people effectively. They probably feel threatened by their lack of knowledge. If you really want to improve your skills as a manager, then you will need to note how you may be communicating with your body language.

Consider the following suggestions and remember it is not what you *think* you are communicating, it is what people are *seeing* and *receiving* that gets your message across.

When people don't jell it is likely to be because a vital ingredient is missing: rapport. Rapport enables you to put people at their ease, gives you an instant insight into how they are feeling, enables you to communicate more effectively and generates a feeling of warmth and trust. With a little effort on your part you can go a long way towards acquiring this skill.

In order to create rapport with your body you need to 'mirror' the other person's body language. Take, for example, an interview. The interviewee enters your office obviously nervous. Their body language reflects how they are feeling. When asked to sit down they will perch on the edge of the chair, cross their legs, clutch their briefcase to their body and avoid eye contact. Their whole demeanour radiates tenseness. You will instantly observe all these signs and begin to put the person at ease, initially by using the 'mirroring' technique to create rapport.

After the initial introductions are over, try sitting with *your* legs crossed, slightly to the front of *your* chair, keeping *your* arms slightly in front of your body. Almost as though you were looking into a mirror and copying the interviewee's posture and gestures, but to a *lesser* degree. Now you are both in a posture which actually creates a 'block' to good communication, and this needs to be rectified tactfully.

Now try to lead the interviewee into a more relaxed frame of mind by gently unwinding *your* body. As unobtrusively as possible, uncross your legs, sit well back on your chair, let your arms drop more to the side and initiate eye contact. Now you are in what is termed as being in a state of 'openness', inviting the interviewee to be more relaxed and responsive to the situation because, and this is the surprising thing, as your body language becomes more 'open', it is highly probably that theirs will too.

Now you are well on the way to creating rapport. Keep as attentive as possible and sit facing the interviewee, readily accepting eye contact. Keep your body language open. A further way of creating rapport is to try to use the same tone or speed of voice as the other person does when talking to them. This can be difficult between genders, but nontheless it is possible. If someone is speaking very quickly and you speak very slowly, there is likely to be little rapport. Also, if they have a high-pitched voice and yours is low and deep, there will be little rapport. This is not to say you should mimic the other person, but be aware of slightly modulating your tone and speed as best you can. When people have rapport, you will often hear their voice tones change in harmony with each other.

Be mindful of your voice; perhaps it would create a more relaxed atmosphere if you lowered your tone, adjusted the volume and responded slightly more slowly than you would if you were in a more fraught situation. Try to change your voice to harmonize (but within reason).

Apart from the voice, consider also the language used. If you are interviewing someone and you ask them, 'What do you *think* about ...' and they reply, 'Well, I feel that ...', then you are likely to think that they are not answering your question. Equally, if you are asked questions by the interviewee and omit to use their language, they may think that you don't understand, or you are not on the same wavelength.

Remember, in most communications the breakdown is:

content	7%
voice	38%
body language	55%

This is why paying attention to what you do rather than what you say can be so effective. Thirteen times more information is available in your non-verbal communication than in your words. Enrich your people-management skills by paying attention to your non-verbal communications and remember that practice makes perfect. Liking people is not necessarily a prerequisite for creating rapport and a little effort on your part could increase this skill considerably.

In order to create rapport, smile initially, for there is nothing better than your looking relaxed in order to relax the other person. So how do we relax other people and demonstrate 'accepting' body language?

Ten thoughts on creating rapport

1. Smile

2. Keep warm eye contact

3. Be natural – the dance of rapport comes easily

4. Mirror the other person's body language initially

5. Open up your body position, look relaxed in order to relax the other person

6. Use appropriate language

7. Adopt voice level and speed in harmony with theirs

8. Value what is being said, even if you disagree

9. Highlight what the other person has said, recognizing that it is their true perspective

10. Give feedback

■ SUMMARY

Now there may be many reasons for certain body postures, but remember the interviewee cannot read your mind, they can only go by what they see. If you disbelieve the validity of body language, then test it out. See how you can relax people by being open yourself.

Try to 'fake it till you make it'; even though you may feel anxious about the interview, don't let the interviewee know. Place your body in a positive position and soon your psyche will follow. The psyche does not know the difference between fantasy and reality. If you think positively, your body reacts accordingly and you will feel confident and at ease. The reverse is also true; think negatively and your body, reacting to fear and anxiety, will produce too much adrenalin, which in turn will result in negative physical symptoms such as palpitations, sweating, or an overwhelming desire to run to the loo.

So remember that trying to achieve rapport with someone is difficult, especially if you don't like them. It is often easier if you get on with someone, but this is not necessarily essential for creating rapport. Rapport means that people are more likely to communicate with you more easily, and establishing rapport creates an environment of confidence, involvement and, hopefully, trust. Trust, of course, is difficult to achieve, especially if you have ever trusted a person and that trust has been broken. No matter how hard you may both attempt to regain the same level of trust, it is virtually impossible after going through the experience of being let down, rejected or even betrayed.

Finally, note carefully all the different types of body language that have been described in this chapter. You can learn far more than you realize and it will help you to understand people better both at work and at home. Of all the body talk that I have addressed, I believe that the foot-turned-upwards is the biggest give-away for you as an interviewer, for you will know that you have asked an uncomfortable question or that the interviewee is feeling uncomfortable with what they are saying. Watch politicians, royalty and celebrities being interviewed and what what happens to their feet – it can be a big give-away!

CHAPTER  **3**

Six thoughts when interviewing

1. Will the setting affect the interview process?

Yes. Think about interviews where you have been the candidate, sitting isolated, surrounded by a horseshoe of often distant, serious looking professionals.

Diagram 1

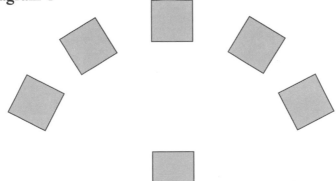

Can you recall how you felt, or feel now as you visualize the scene? One after another, looking at you, sometimes from a greater height, questioning you. Sometimes the questions are so complicated and convoluted that it is difficult to understand what is being asked – let alone answer and remain feeling positive while sitting alone against the opposition.

Even when the interviewer is skilled at questioning, such a setting will be daunting. Isolating the chair can make people feel very threatened. After all, courts use the witness box to isolate and create pressure on the witness, defendant, persecutor or allegedly guilty party.

So decide on the outcome you want and, if you want to get the best out of the person, think positively about how the setting will affect them. Ideally, if the purpose of the interview necessitates several people being involved, then opt for a round table. This gives a feeling of equality and involvement, not of status, financial reward, influence or power. People are equal in how they feel – hurt, pressurized, prized, valued – regardless of status or prestige.

Group dynamics often significantly affect the way in which people behave or respond. Consider your home setting when entertaining guests for a meal. Do you consider the dynamics of who sits next to whom so that individuals do not feel left out? Do you have a long narrow table at which people sit facing one another but are unable to interact with everyone? If you ever have to buy a new table, then go for a round or an oval one and you will experience much more involvement and the inclusion of all concerned.

Diagram 2

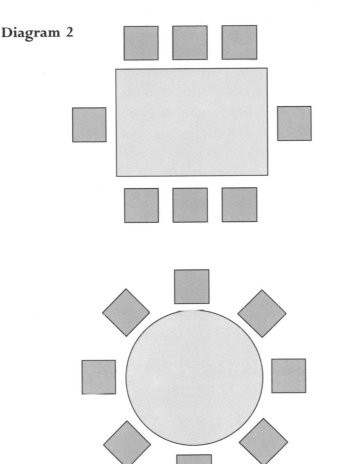

Interviews are actually possible without tables. Where there are no tables, you will be far more intimate with the interviewee. Remember to get rid of the 'death chair': that is the one chair that is left because someone has not turned up, or is late. It may be surprising, but, knowingly or unknowingly, people will be using up their 'mental energy' thinking about the space in terms such as, 'I've organized myself to be here on time, but they couldn't be bothered'.

Have you ever thought about your managerial room and how it may affect your interaction with your staff? Where is your desk? Do you sit behind it, facing the door? Do you have a larger chair facing a smaller one? Are you on show? Can you be seen by other colleagues through glass?

Let us talk ideally, because I guess some of you can manage people without a desk, while others may have or need a powerful looking desk or an office where they can feel secure.

A typical authoritarian, formal manager would be likely to have the following set up:

Diagram 3

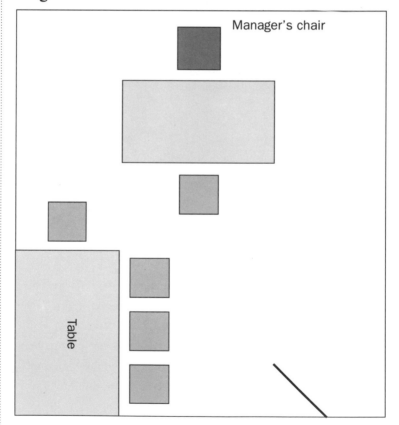

Manager's chair

Table

A manager who wants to get the best out of his or her staff is more likely to recognize and be sensitive to the influence of their room setting on others:

Diagram 4

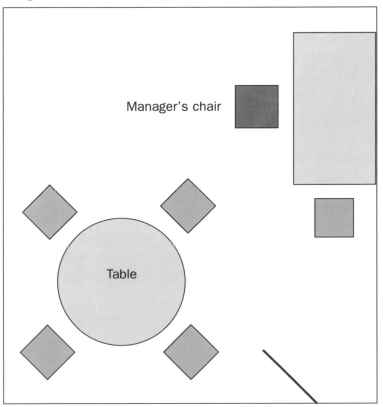

This setting offers equality around a low coffee table. At the same time you could work at your desk near a window, which can help you to clear your thinking and expand your thoughts. It has a chair where someone can face you for a brief chat. You can have a limited 'open-door' recognized policy if you wish.

So, having decided on the physical setting suitable for a one-to-one interview, choose two similar chairs which face each other. No desk in between. This is not just for informal interviews, it is also better for appraisals. Remember, there is no such thing in job interviews as 'an informal interview'. Your performance and impression given during the day will be reported back to the appointing group.

Now let us think about other influences. Do you have prints, posters, plants, ornaments, books, certificates, photographs on display? Have you ever considered what these room accoutrements are saying about you?

You may have posters that suggest your politics, religion or beliefs which may be offensive to others. Even your pictures or your display of trophies and awards may upset some of your colleagues.

I recall one woman complaining bitterly about a sexual sculpture that was, in her perception, dominant in a male interviewer's room. She considered him to be a male chauvinist. This was not my experience of the man involved. Later I visited his room and could empathize with how she may have felt. Unfortunately, he had that day been given the sculpture in order to return it to its owner, who lived near to him. It had been kept by a female colleague for temporary safe keeping during maternity leave, but its owner had subsequently decided not to return to work. The statue had been placed on a windowsill behind him, but in full view of the interviewee.

Is your room chaotic? Chaos is contagious. Your desk needs to be cleared. No, it does not mean that you haven't enough to do, it means that you are organized. A clear desk means a clear desk, no pending tray – put any pending paper away in the drawer, even if that means emptying all the rubbish out of your desk drawers.

Be aware of any off-putting odours that may hang around your room, or around you. Does your room smell of musty dampness? Are you surrounded by a halo of bad breath, tobacco, sweaty feet, body odour or, maybe, too much garlic the night before? All this can be very distracting for an interviewee and will certainly not help to create a comfortable atmosphere. Do be aware, however, that the excessively strong perfume of air freshener or pot pourri can have a similarly adverse affect on people.

So be aware of the messages that your room setting is giving out and also ensure that you won't be disturbed, whatever the reason, during the interview. For counselling, disciplining, appraising, delegating, praising, you still need to be undisturbed. Transfer your telephone calls, put up a 'please do not disturb' sign, relax and enjoy the rapport and the motivation of a positive interview.

2. Remember to use the three-minute rule

Whatever type of interview you are taking part in you will need the following range of skills, but first let us remember the 'three-minute rule'. We can safely say that impressions gained during the first three minutes of any interview are crucial to the outcome, both from the point of view of the interviewee and the interviewer. Decisions are made about each other during this time and often the rest of the interview is simply used to confirm these first impressions. Remember, you never get a second chance to make a first impression.

If you still need convincing of the importance of the 'three-minute rule' in a job interview and how it can set the scene for what is to follow, try to relate the same principle to home situations, one of which has probably happened to you at one time or another.

How many of us have arrived home from the office feeling really gloomy and sorry for ourselves, having used up so much of our mental energy dealing with people at work and being pleasant to individuals that you do not actually like? 'Poor me', we think, 'See how tired I look, and it's all because I've been working so hard and none of it's appreciated.' Automatically the posture becomes stooped and the face sags into a picture of misery. The first words uttered are 'I've had a terrible day at the office, and I'm really fed-up!' Later you may begin to feel brighter and expect your partner to respond to your new, positive mood, but then you're surprised that they don't. Despite feeling pleasure at the thought of your arriving home from work, they are probably now feeling quite dejected and unable to relate to your more communicative mood. You have lost the chance of a good evening because of your initial inter-action with the person you care about. Test it out and see what happens.

Back at work, what other tips are there for the inter-viewer? To begin with, recognize the importance of the first three minutes when you meet someone, however familiar or unfamiliar they are to you. Let us take a job interview for example. If you shake someone's hand with a limp wrist or a steel grip, then psychologically you are likely to affect the person. They may think that you are a bit drippy in the first instance, or aggressive in the second response.

■ Shake hands firmly, thumb-up-to-thumb.

If you smile too much or look too severe, the result is a feel-ing of unease in the other person. Remember:

'Powerful people smile when pleased
Powerless people smile to please'

■ Offer an open face, free of scowls and with a genuine smile to put people at their ease.

If you avoid eye contact you will run the risk of appearing either sly or shy. Neither perception is useful.

■ Look straight at the person, neither aggressively nor sensually, but openly, honestly and directly.

If you are nervous and reflect this in your body movements, your anxiety will be transmitted to the other person.

■ Keep as still as you can, depending on where the first three minutes of the interview take place. Remember, you can empower yourself if you stand up instead of sitting down, that is, when first being introduced or welcoming someone to an interview.

Beware of negative opening remarks, since these will directly affect the emotions of the other person. For instance, if, even with a firm handshake, open face and positive body posture, your first words are, 'I see you're late!' or 'Oh dear! I'm late!', then a cloud of negativity will immediately descend on the proceedings.

■ Think about a positive opening comment to get the interview under way: 'I am so pleased to meet you' or, 'I'm pleased you could make it today'.

3. Dealing with negative people

It is likely that some of your staff will be highly motivated while others may behave negatively. Some will talk about how stressed they are when, perhaps, they have little to do, while others seem to take on a great deal of work and yet see the pressure as something which actually motivates and excites them.

One of the skills needed in order to deal with negative staff is the ability to reframe what they are saying. This is 'reframing', not rephrasing.

While some staff will maintain that they are stressed when they are not, others will deny being stressed, using language like 'it's exciting' or 'what a wonderful opportunity to ...' Eventually, you will recognize that some people sound negative but may not be, whereas others may be negative but in fact may have the ability to use the right kind of positive language. So let us look briefly at how language can create stress and also how you can reframe what you are saying when talking to a member of staff, in order to get the best out of them.

Language reframing

Our language can create stress in others or inform people how stressed we are. We may use battle language, 'I fought for the section', 'the swords were out'; or catastrophic language 'it was a nightmare', 'the effects will be horrendous', 'no one's job will be safe'.

One way of handling stress is to learn to 'reframe' your language. By this I mean turning negative thoughts or statements into positive statements. For example, your line manager says to you, 'I would like you to take over the administration of this particular project because you are a good administrator'. You reply 'Yes, OK' (but really you want to say NO).

Thought

There he/she goes again, always asking me to do the paper work. Why do I always get lumbered instead of the other staff around me?'

Reframing:

> It feels really good that I am considered to be so capable, however, I must ensure that if I take on this extra administration then I will have to drop some other area of work, otherwise I will overload myself. Also I could ask my line manager to indicate which of my workloads he/she thinks is my priority.

Now think of some situation that could happen or has happened to you at work where you feel or felt negative.

_____

_____

_____

What was your initial extra response?

_____

_____

_____

Now try and 'reframe' your natural responses:

_____

_____

_____

What a wonderful opportunity to ...

A reframing technique is to start a sentence with 'What a great opportunity to ...', so if something happens that is unexpected, inconvenient, hurtful or difficult, one is prepared and able to reduce one's stress and create a feeling of wellbeing.

Let us start with today. Whatever frame of mind you are in at present, begin the day by completing the following phrase:

What a great opportunity to

_____

_____

_____

4. Ensure that people understand and remember what you are trying to say to them

Giving and receiving feedback

Assumptions are the killers of relationships. It is vital that you learn how to give and receive feedback. However good a manager you are, people cannot read your mind, so tell them what you think and ask for feedback about your own performance. In order to get the best out of your staff, you will need to be able to give them feedback and to stop assuming that they know how you feel and what you think about them.

You may believe that your staff are aware that you value their work or that they should know how effective or ineffective they are in their job, but they won't know unless you tell them. If your response to this is 'they know if they are not doing their job properly because I tell them' – assuming that if they are not told they are doing badly then they must realize that they are doing well – you need to think again. People need to be told that they are working well, absence of criticism won't be read as positive feedback. Even the most confident people need to know that their work is appreciated and prized.

In this section I will begin by showing you a model of how feedback helps both you and your staff to recognize unused potential, followed by guidelines on how both to give and receive feedback.

The Johari Window

The Johari model* was initially designed as a way of understanding how feedback skills can be improved. It also demonstrates how you can relate more effectively to people by revealing some information about your private self and asking for feedback about your 'blind' self.

It helps managers to understand quickly what is happening to them and their staff. If used correctly, it is a useful tool for both the first-time manager and the experienced manager.

Diagram 5: The Johari Window

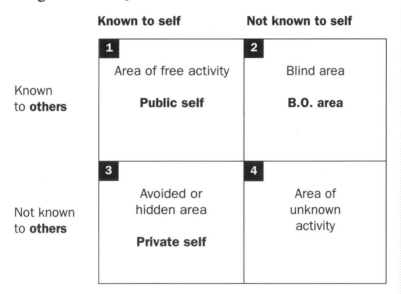

	Known to self	Not known to self
Known to **others**	**1** Area of free activity **Public self**	**2** Blind area **B.O. area**
Not known to **others**	**3** Avoided or hidden area **Private self**	**4** Area of unknown activity

* *The Johari Window* by Joe Kurtz and Harry Ingham

The process of giving and receiving feedback happens in all interviews and in any interaction with your staff. It allows a real understanding of relationships and a valuable exchange of views.

Under conditions of **self disclosure**

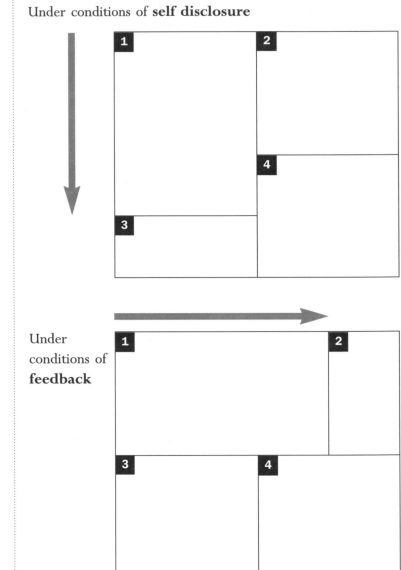

Under conditions of **feedback**

Under conditions of **feedback & self disclosure**

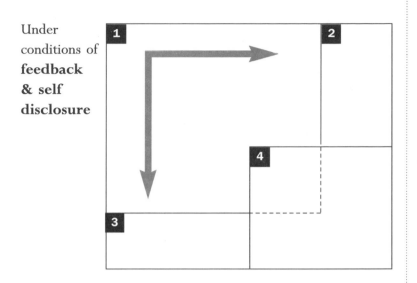

Look at these three Johari Window diagrams. They set the scene as to how we give and receive feedback. First of all you will see that there are areas that you know about yourself and that your members of staff know about you. This is called the public self.

The public self

This may cover aspects of your background; your qualifications; your personality; how you are likely to react in certain situations; what motivates you; whether you are ambitious or not; whether you are supportive or not; whether, in fact, you like them or not. It is only when knowledge of this 'public self' is increased that you can attain a better relationship with your staff, and you do this by revealing aspects of your 'private self'.

The private self

The 'private self' is about your self-perceptions, your knowledge, your experience, things that you are unlikely to share with everybody, possibly even areas that you are ashamed of, would censor, or wonder if they are actually applicable to the working relationship. Perhaps aspects of your personal life, your relationships and partnerships would fall into this category. By revealing some of your 'private self' to a member of your staff, either at an interview or appraisal, you have actually pushed the public 'window' wider. So you may choose to say things like, 'I also have difficulties in that area' or, 'I've been concerned about that particular aspect'. You may even, from this private self, apologize and say, 'I have been concerned about the fact that I have not been giving you sufficient support' or, 'I notice you don't seem to talk to me as often as you did'.

The blind self

You also have a blind side, or a 'blind self' and that refers to aspects of yourself that are known to other people, but of which you are totally unaware. You have no idea how your staff think about you or feel about you unless they tell you or you ask them. However good a manager you are, you cannot read their minds. It is up to you actually to ask for feedback.

It is up to you to say, 'How do you see me?', 'In what ways can I help?', 'How do you feel the meeting went?' The replies may be surprising and upsetting, and the relationship will have to be good if your staff are to be honest in their replies. It is nonetheless a most valuable exercise. By getting feedback from your staff as to how you are behaving, and as to how you are perceived to be managing your section/department/group/team, you will be able to become more self-aware. You may, in fact, have very good motives behind your actions. But it is how people see you, not how you think you are being seen, that matters and what other *people* think you have said, not what *you* think you have said, that will have an effect. By enlarging the 'public window' and receiving feedback about your 'blind self', you will move into the unused potential or your 'secret area'.

The secret area (unused potential)

By receiving feedback you can perhaps recognize ways in which you could change, ways in which you are behaving that may be causing offence, ways in which you are speaking that may be causing anxiety among your staff. Perhaps you can remember being told when you were small that you were good at something, but you didn't actually know it until you were told? You may in your career have been advised or motivated to take on a new job because someone said, 'this job is just for you' or, 'why don't you apply for it?' or, 'I'm going to give you this particular area of responsibility because I recognize that you have these qualities'. This positive information will give you the encouragement you need. It will give you the ability to work towards a better job, maybe involving more responsibility, power, influence or job satisfaction.

As you receive feedback, so you can give it to your staff in order to develop their unused potential. This is what the process is about, and you need to understand it.

Some people find it difficult to give feedback. They revert to, 'well, I'd better not say any more', 'I don't want to upset their feelings' or, 'it will go away'. This is the reaction of an ostrich-like manager. You and your staff will work better together if you are in an open, honest relationship.

Try to think about feedback as receiving a present. Sometimes, of course, we open presents and say, 'Just what I wanted', like the sixth pair of socks for Christmas to go with the five sets of hankies, when in fact it is something you dislike intensely. Likewise, some feedback can be very painful, but again, learning itself can be painful. By being given feed-back you become self-aware. You are then able to make the choice of whether you are going to do anything about this knowledge or remain as you are. It takes a good manager to recognize that there are ways in which he or she can improve, develop and be more effective. So when you are given this present of feedback, see it as something that will help you to grow.

When you give feedback to your staff, start off with the ground rule that anything you are feeding back is based on the fundamental concept of being supportive and not ultra-critical. You are giving your staff feedback because of the regard you have for them; because you are actually bothering to do so; because you want to see them improve; because you want to see them grow. Give the feedback in such a way that it is understandable. Be succinct, don't go all around the houses.

Always, in feedback, find something positive to begin with. For example, 'You are really good at dealing with cus-tomers and working with your colleagues. However, I'm concerned that there are times when you don't appear to smile very much or have a great deal of energy.' If you start giving feedback by saying something positive, 'You're really good at that', and then go on to say, 'but...', people will inevitably be waiting with a sinking heart for the 'but'. Try instead using the word 'although'. They may also be waiting for this word and see it as meaning the same as 'but'; all the same it is still a little gentler when you are adding critical feedback.

After you have offered criticism you may need to ask for feedback, although people may not readily give it to you because you may be more powerful and influential than they are, since you are in a position where you could hire or fire them. You must give people permission to be honest with you. You need to free your staff to be able to give you feedback without the fear that in the future you will use it as a stick to beat them with.

Never ask a question if you are not prepared to listen carefully to the answer. If you do not want to grow from feedback, then stay wrapped up in your little shell, but it is amazing how useful feedback can be. You will certainly manage people more effectively by becoming aware of what perceptions your staff have of you.

Equally, your staff will be better off if they receive feedback from you. Do remember, you can give feedback without any criticism at the end. Remember to praise your staff and tell them how much you value them. Make sure you say 'well done' and 'thank you' at the right moment.

5. Transactional analysis

Transactional analysis is a term well known to many managers. It offers a way of thinking about how people speak from different 'ego' states or different attitudes. Sometimes what is important is not *what* people say, but *how* they say it, and interpreting the real meaning will help form good relationships. The language that is used can give you an insight into which 'ego' state someone is speaking from.

Sometimes we discount people when they do pay us compliments. In Transactional Analysis terms, compliments are called 'warm fuzzies' because they make us feel good and warm and fuzzy all over. On the other hand, criticisms are called 'cold pricklies' because they make us feel cold, prickly and put-down. When you are complimented do you do any of the following? For example, when a person says, 'Well done, I really appreciate you getting that project back on time', do you reply 'Well, if I had more time, I could have done it better', if someone says 'You're looking really good today', do you reply, 'Well, I don't know why – I'm absolutely tired out'. By replying in this manner you are discounting the compliment. Another way of discounting what people say is to give your praise away to someone else, 'You did that really well' and you reply, 'Oh, my partner helped me'. Or you give the praise back to the person: 'You are great at reception' and you reply, 'So are you'.

If you are given positive feedback and keep discounting it in this way, people will eventually stop giving it to you. It is important to learn to accept it – all you need to say is 'Thank you'.

6. Sometimes I find it difficult to relate to some staff when interviewing or talking to them

As a manager it will be difficult for you to be spontaneous, open and effective every day because of things that may be happening to you at home, or pressures that you may have at work. However, you are paid to manage and to get the best out of your staff.

Sometimes simply referring to a checklist will enable you to recall some of the ways in which you may be proficient, or areas which you need to rethink.

So let us have a look at some simple check points which can help you to relate more effectively to your staff and encourage them to work to their full potential.

20 WAYS TO RELATE TO YOUR STAFF MORE EFFECTIVELY

1   Listen more and talk less.

2   Understand the content and feelings behind the words. Empathize with their world. Walk in your staff's shoes, see from their frame of reference, listen through their ears, see through their eyes.

3   Relax. Instead of thinking what you have to say, concentrate on what your staff are saying. Some people have to say something, others speak only when they have something to say. Try to tune in to their body postures, their movements, their gestures, their breathing. We only remember 7 per cent of content, 38 per cent of voice and 55 per cent of someone's body language. There is thirteen times more information available in non-verbal communication than in words.

4   Ask people open questions. Invite them to expand on what they are saying. Entrenched views tend to disappear when you gain more information from people. Avoid self-disclosure, when it is about you wanting to join in rather than sharing information. Never ask 'why?'. Remember that it forces the person to explain, defend or justify their reasons.

5   Stay with silences. Do not rush into what you want to say.

6   When you talk, make sure that what you want to say is helpful to the other person. Avoid the impulse to be clever or put people down. Avoid being judgemental and critical. Watch your language; use working 'with' rather than 'for'.

7   Smile and keep eye contact, making encouraging moves and sounds. Recognize the importance of how you use your body, remembering any cultural differences. Avoid gestures above your shoulders, which disempower you.

8   Say what you have to say simply, briefly and succinctly.

9   Reflect upon what is being said. Check out what you are hearing and what is being understood.

10 Address the issue, not the individual.

11 If you do not agree with someone, simply say 'I do not agree'. Remember it is possible to disagree without being disagreeable.

12 If you are uncomfortable with someone, try to find out who they may be reminding you of, recognizing that you may actually be projecting feelings on to them that don't belong to them but are about you.

13 Value what other people have to say, but remember that you are responsible towards your staff, not for them.

14 Allow people to finish their sentences, don't finish sentences for them. Own your statements: say 'I' when talking about yourself, rather than using 'we' or 'us' or 'you' or 'them'.

15 Be assertive, not aggressive or passive. Remember, if you always do what you have always done, then you will always get what you have always got, so try something new. Learning can be painful but it is worthwhile. Assertive behaviour makes you more confident, more open and more honest.

16 It is all right to have fun, so let loose that spontaneous fun-loving child in you. Stop being afraid of embarrassing yourself.

17 If you only want one answer, don't ask the question. Be prepared for people to answer in the way they want to, not in the way in which you want them to reply.

18 Reframe negative viewpoints. Instead of saying, 'I am bored by this meeting', say, 'I need to make meetings more lively and interesting'. It is your responsibility to do that also with your staff.

19 The best way to achieve rapport is to take your cue from the other person by mirroring their body language and recognizing their viewpoint.

20 Offer staff feedback when they would like it and ask people for feedback. This is not a list of compliments, it will actually provide learning both ways.

QUESTIONNAIRE 4

What can you do now?

Having read this chapter, test your memory and see if you have any new thoughts on interviewing.

1   How would you set out a room for:
    A job interview? _____

    _____

    A meeting of six people? _____

    _____

A one-to-one interview? _____

_____

2 What aspects of the room might adversely affect the interview?

_____

_____

3 What would you try to do in the first three minutes of an interview?

_____

_____

4 What is the difference between reframing and rephrasing?

_____

_____

5 What is meant by the 'public self'?

_____

6 What is meant by the 'private self'?

_____

7 What is meant by the 'blind self'?

_____

8 What is meant by someone's secret area?

_____

9 What are the reasons for giving feedback to staff?

_____

_____

_____

10 What three things could you do to relate better to your staff?

_____

_____

_____

CHAPTER

How can I appraise staff effectively to get the best out of them?

D one well, appraisals can motivate, focus and empower your staff. Badly done, they can disillusion, frustrate and devalue them.

Whether you work in an organization that has a very impressive, elaborate appraisal policy, or one that favours a much more relaxed attitude towards staff reviews and appraisal, it is highly probable that at some point in your working life you will need to sit down with a member of your staff and appraise them. It is worth remembering, though, that however detailed or deficient your company policy is, appraisal aims are of little or no use if you cannot actually put them into practice.

The appraisee will need to be asked about their successes, their need for support, aspirations and targets and also be given the opportunity to give you feedback about YOUR performance. Remember, properly conducted appraisals are a two-way flow of information, although ideally the appraiser should take up only 10 per cent of the talking time.

Appraisals can often go wrong if the appraiser and appraisee actually have conflicting agendas. As a manager you need to let people know exactly where they stand; recognize their good work; be able to highlight any difficulties they may be experiencing owing to their own lack of skill; discuss any problems they may be having with other members of staff and, if necessary, with you. You will need to illuminate the direction in which they need to go in order to improve and develop their present tasks.

You will have to set work targets and, where possible, talk about any promotions that may be imminent: possibly there may be a desire on the appraisee's part to move on to a job with more responsibility or more pay. Do let people know how they will progress in the system. The ability of a manager to assess a member of staff's need for improvement as well as to celebrate their successes is essential.

You need to be clear about your motives for appraisal. If it is thought that it is solely about making more profit, then you are unlikely to get the best out of the interview for the appraisee. It is important to remember that appraisal is not about confrontation, not an opportunity to handle conflict, and not a chance to discipline. These factors are on-going, and as such need to be dealt with by you as and when they happen throughout the year.

In this chapter we will look at appraisal skills; appraisal frameworks; how to initiate, implement, or act on an appraisal system; the preparation for the interview, the interview itself and specific questions; the setting of targets and what happens after the interview.

Now complete Questionnaire 5, which highlights the need for thinking about several aspects of an appraisal system.

QUESTIONNAIRE 5

● ●

Twenty-five considerations when setting up or implementing an appraisal scheme:

1 What are your key objectives and purposes for introducing or having an appraisal scheme?

_____

_____

_____

2 How will the scheme be managed and over what time-scale?

_____

_____

_____

3 Who has responsibility for designing the scheme?

_____

4 Who has responsibility for implementing the scheme?

_____

5 How will the appraisees be selected and who will be the appraisers?

_____

_____

6   What training will the appraisers and appraisees need?

_____

_____

7   How will it be done?

_____

_____

8   Who will do the training?

_____

9   How will the scheme be monitored and by whom?

_____

_____

10   How many staff do you think one manager can effectively appraise?

_____

11   What appeal mechanism should there be?, e.g. the right to choose your appraiser or appraisee or express concerns about the process.

_____

_____

12   How frequently will appraisal interviews take place?

_____

13   How is the scheme to be communicated to staff?

_____

_____

14   Which staff will be involved in the scheme?

_____

15   When will interviews take place?

_____

16 Where will interviews take place?

_____

17 Who will design the forms that will be used by the appraiser and the appraisee?

_____

18 What other ways of collecting evidence on performance will be used?

_____

_____

19 Who will appraise the managing director?

_____

20 What do you foresee will be the most likely areas of difficulty you will encounter?

_____

_____

_____

21 How can these areas of difficulty best be resolved?

_____

_____

_____

22 Who will have access to the documentation?

_____

23 Will there be confidential documents and, if so, where will they be kept and who will have access to them?

_____

_____

_____

24 What resources does your organization have for
implementing the scheme?

_____

_____

25 How will you ensure acceptable and measurable targets
are set for individuals?

_____

_____

How to manage or implement an appraisal scheme

Appraisals can be a wonderful opportunity for your staff to
focus on their job and make plans to develop their unused
potential. They can also provide an opportunity for you to get
the best out of your staff in two ways: first as an individual,
and second, as a team member.

If you are embarking on an appraisal system, you need to
ascertain some formalities and make some decisions before
you begin. Even if you are already involved in a scheme, you
need to consider what you want to achieve and how you are
going to achieve it.

First of all, you need to decide on your key objectives and
the real purpose of the scheme. Ideally, it should be a supportive framework that aids staff development. Done against a
background of redundancies, or for pure profit or competitive
edge alone, you will create fear and alienate your staff.

Decide on how the scheme is going to be managed. In
order to do this it is essential that all the senior managers are
committed to the importance of the practice. The ideal time-
scale for formal appraisals is annual.

The person responsible for designing the scheme and

producing the necessary forms needs to have insight and knowledge of the people within the organizational structure. Also, he or she must know the possible needs of staff at all levels. However, the person responsible for implementing and/or monitoring the scheme needs to be someone who is sensible, able and understanding. Many staff are highly suspicious of appraisals, some considering them as little more than a way of reducing the work force. So choose someone to whom staff could go if they were concerned about their appointed appraiser or appraisal interview.

Design a scheme that indicates who will be appraising whom. This needs great tact and sensitivity. First, remember that no manager can effectively appraise (or manage, in fact) more than seven or eight people. So in chosing appraisers keep this in mind. If several staff are expected to be appraised by someone they dislike, or by managers with whom they do not share any values or beliefs, then your scheme will go awry. Even one member in such a position may affect how others may respond to the process. Hence you will need to have some form of appeal mechanism.

Having decided on your policy and who will appraise which members of staff, you need to communicate this in the simplest possible way. Avoid lengthy documents – few people will read them. Staff need to know who will appraise them and why, how, where and when. Most organizations choose a person's line manager to be the appraiser. This can be seen as an opportunity or a threat, so establish an appeals procedure.

There can be many reasons for someone not wishing to be interviewed by their delegated appraiser. There may be a lack of trust or respect, the interviewee may think that the person delegated is incapable, or there may be, or may have been, a sexual involvement or a relationship that has broken down. Some staff may resent their line manager because he or she secured the job for which they had applied. So be sensitive to these possibilities.

Interviews should preferably take place on neutral ground at a mutually satisfactory time. Avoid doing more than two appraisals in one day, since you are likely to merge the experiences.

Some appraisals may involve the disclosure of confidential information, so it is vital that you jointly decide what is written on records, where these will be kept and who will be allowed access to them.

Whether you are in the process of instigating a system or are already involved in one, you will need to ensure that training is given to both appraisers and appraisees. In-house training with a sensitive and humorous trainer can help to change people's attitude towards the policy. It can reduce insecurity and unite staff in recognizing the positive elements of appraisal. You can do this at the training course by asking delegates 'What did you think or feel about the appraisal?' before the training took place and 'What do you think about it now?'

It is essential that your appraisal training is skill-focused, which means including acquiring the practical skill of active listening. Many people think that they listen, but they don't. It should also include the arts of how to reflect what is being heard, the importance and use of body language, the asking of open questions, giving feedback and the setting of targets.

The training needs to conclude by staging an appraisal. One way would be to offer a three-person exercise, let us say A, B and C:

A	Appraiser
B	Appraised
C	What is happening

All three will give feedback to each other and then each person takes on a different letter. I say letter rather than role as many people fear 'role play'. A good trainer would explain that you are not playing a role but being yourself when being appraised, appraising, interviewing or observing. Be sure to find an experienced and effective trainer. The best way is usually by recommendation. A bad training experience can create havoc with your best-laid plans and systems.

Preparation for the interview

Let us now look at the appraisal interview, starting with the preparation involved. What do you need to do before the interview?

In preparation, you need to organize a time-slot suitable for both parties several days before the interview. Allow a minimum of one-and-a-half hours. Appraisals that last longer stop becoming appraisals and start becoming just a general chat. The following suggestions are, of course, based upon ideal situations, although it is recognized that very often it will not be possible to achieve this.

Ideally the appraisal should take part on neutral ground, that is, a place where you will both feel at ease and certainly will not be interrupted. The way the room is organized for the appraisal may seem self-evident, but it can make a big difference to the effectiveness of the interview. You will need two chairs of the same height which will face each other, maybe a coffee table in between, but really it is best to have nothing in the room which may interrupt the rapport that you can create as the interviewer.

Beforehand you need to agree with the appraisee what paperwork needs to be exchanged, and it is worthwhile to prepare and assemble any other written information about the member of staff that may be helpful to you. Remember to do some pre-reading and select key areas to cover mutual and individual issues for discussion, not forgetting to ask the appraisee for their suggestions when settling upon the topics which you would both like to discuss.

Adequate preparation is vitally important for a successful appraisal or interview and in many organizations it is normal for appraiser and appraisee to meet prior to the main interview in order to discuss the areas that they are likely to want to explore in more depth.

It is often thought that you need to know a lot about the employee's work in order to appraise them, but I disagree with this. I think you can actually appraise people without having a detailed knowledge of the intricacies of their work – other specialists can know that.

With good interview skills you are able to deal with all aspects that are relevant to the work situation, and mutual benefit should be gained as a result of discussing aspirations, satisfactions, frustrations and needs within the workplace. Of course, if you are familiar with the actual type of work, this would enable you to have a greater understanding of what the issues are, but it is more important that you have interviewing skills, rather than knowledge of the area of work.

The appraisal interview

Having dealt with all the preparation necessary, you are now ready to appraise your member of staff. Your aim should be to reduce any fear and hostility towards the process, and to emphasize the positive side of appraisal.

The first, and possibly most important skill you need to

acquire, is that of putting someone at their ease and creating some degree of rapport. As discussed earlier, there are a number of techniques you can call upon to help create this feeling of ease: by using effective body language, for example, by 'mirroring'; by actively listening with eyes, ears and heart; by asking open questions; and by using similar language to that of the interviewee.

During the appraisal it is important to recognize that while you are endeavouring to establish rapport with a member of staff, there will be people with whom you will feel immediately comfortable, and others who will create anxiety in you. Try not to project your anxiety back to them.

Look and listen effectively. Make a mental note of the content, meaning, emotions and the non-verbal signs that you are picking up.

During the interview it is better if you do not take notes, as both you and the appraisee may find this distracting. You will already have read all their details before the interview, so this time should be spent in face-to-face interaction. If you say that the note-taking is to help you to remember, then you need to improve your memory skills. If you cannot remember things, it is unlikely that you will act on them. This is the time when you can sum up mutually what targets have been agreed, prior to writing them down, but the member of staff needs your undivided attention when he or she is being appraised.

If neither of you can remember what targets had been decided, because you were not writing it down, then there is little chance that targets will be achieved. It is better if you deal with target-setting towards the end of the appraisal interview so you will both have to remember any targets for only about ten minutes – hence you should be able to recall the significant points of discussion without notes.

How can I question staff without them feeling threatened or patronized?

When questioning people it is important to recognize that certain questions will bring particular types of information and responses, so it is essential for you to recognize what these different types of questions are. Before interviewing a member of staff it is worth considering the following types of questions:

Open question

The advantage of an open question is that it cannot be answered with a one-word answer, such as 'yes' or 'no'. It is the most useful type of question available to you if you are trying to get the best out of people. For example, you may say, 'Tell me about it', or, 'What was that about?', or, 'How did you arrive at that conclusion?' Open questioning is non-directive, that is, you are not indicating exactly how you want the question answered and it is, therefore, an excellent tool to use if you wish to get your member of staff talking freely about their ideas and feelings, as well as exploring facts.

Closed questions

Closed questions are likely to be answered by a one-word answer, for instance 'yes' or 'no'. For example, 'I understand from what you say that you are pleased with ...', the answer then being yes or no. Use this technique to summarize a point, or to bring a member of staff back to the topic in question if the conversation has wandered. Closed questions are also a useful way to check if you have understood the main points of the interview correctly.

Specific questions

Specific questions are important if you need to have accurate information. For example, 'When do you think you will be able to finish this work?', or 'Precisely how many will be coming to the event?' Specific questions are used to find out facts and offer a direct approach; they are good for talkative members of staff when you need to pin them down and keep them to the point.

Reflecting

A skill you need to learn is how to reflect what people say so you can test whether you have understood them correctly. It also gives your member of staff the opportunity to know that you have listened to what they have said and have understood the message they have been trying to put across to you. It is also useful for a member of staff to think about what they have been saying, as sometimes they can gain insight by someone else reflecting their thoughts, opinions and feelings. For instance, 'It sounds as though you are happy with ...'

If you reverse a question by rephrasing and sending it back to the member of staff, this keeps the person talking while avoiding personal involvement, or your bias, showing. It can encourage a member of staff to expand the subject further, so by reversing you would say, 'So you are saying that you are not happy with ...' and then they will continue, possibly giving you reasons for what they have stated.

Leading questions

Leading questions direct people towards coming to some kind of solution or agreement. For example, 'I think it is terrible that ...'. The actual answer is being given in the question. This type of question can be very dangerous if used inadvertently, but it is a good way of testing reactions or relaxing a nervous member of staff initially. For example, 'I think your good work is the …'

Hypothetical questions

'If you had someone who …', or, 'If you were in my position what …'. are hypothetical in that they are supposedly made up. However, they are very often thoughts that are actually being explored at the time by either members of staff or management. Otherwise, how would these things spring to mind if they have not already been chewed over? For example, 'If you had somebody who …' or, 'If there were money to spend, what would you initiate?' These questions are testing reactions or solutions to a possible situation and as such can also be very helpful when encouraging staff development.

Having recognized the different types of question that are available to you during an interview, think through what kind of language makes staff feel threatened or patronized. Using words like 'working with' rather than 'working for', avoiding use of the word 'subordinate' or 'boss' 'up', 'down', 'looking up towards', 'delegating down'.

Never use the word 'why?' if you are wanting to encourage a member of staff. This is not to say take 'why' out of your vocabulary, it is an important word, but do not use it if you want to get the best out of your staff. If you were to ask 'Why are you late?', the word 'why?' makes people feel they have to justify themselves, whereas if they were asked 'What happened to make you late?' they are more likely to tell you their reasons.

Useful questions to ask in interviews

■ THE BEGINNING OF THE INTERVIEW

Welcome the appraisee, reassure him or her and set the scene. Offer tea or coffee if you like but do not start the interview until you are both unencumbered. (These openings are also helpful in job interviews.)

Ten useful openings

1 What do you hope for/expect/fear/want/need from this session?

2 How do you feel about this appraisal?

3 What would you say have been your successes or satisfactions over the last year?

4 What areas of your work have disappointed or irritated you?

5 What do you think are your key responsibilities and tasks in your job?

6 What would you like to change?

7 How would you do that?

8 In what ways would a change of emphasis be beneficial, both to you and the organization?

9 Overall how have you felt about your job this year?

10 What frustrations have you had?

■ THE MIDDLE OF THE INTERVIEW

The following questions can be asked in any order. They are simply ideas for areas that you might wish to explore with your member of staff.

Ten opening questions

1   What interests you most about your work?

2   What do you consider are your major assets?

3   In what areas of your work do you need support?

4   In what ways do you feel your potential has been fully used or under-used?

5   Are there any ways you would like to expand your role but which are not available to you or being offered to you?

6   What was the most important or significant success for you over the last year?

7   What support do you require to do your job effectively?

8   What difficulties have you encountered?

9   What did you learn from them?

10 What motivates you?

■ LOOKING AT THE APPRAISEE'S NEEDS AND DEVELOPMENT

Again, these questions can be asked in any kind of order. They concentrate on the development of the appraisee.

Ten opening questions:

1   Where do you see yourself in one year's time?

2   Where do you see yourself in three years' time?

3   What do you think you will need in order to get there?

4   What aspects of your work would you like to change?

5   What staff development or training do you think you might need?

6   What can I do to help that situation?

7   What could your colleagues do to make your work more manageable?

8   Under what conditions do you work best?

9   What aspect of your work would you like to develop for greater job satisfaction?

10   What could you do to make your job more enjoyable?

■ DEALING WITH DIFFICULT ISSUES

At some point you may need to look at any areas of stress, frustration, or conflict your appraisee may be experiencing at work. But, remember that appraisals are *not* set for handling specific conflicts: you need to do this in a separate way on a different occasion.

The following ten questions can be useful ways of handling this and specifying the areas of frustration, stress and conflict. By resolving some of the stress or frustration you are much more likely to get the best out of your staff.

Ten questions

1   What are your frustrations at work?

2   Are there any stresses you would like to talk to me about?

3   What conflicts are you experiencing within yourself?

4   What conflicts are you experiencing with other staff?

5   What conflicts are you experiencing within the organization?

6   What conflicts are you experiencing with our systems or policies?

7   What can I do as your line manager to alleviate some of your frustrations/stresses/conflicts?

8   What could your colleagues do to alleviate some of your frustrations/stresses/conflicts?

9   What do you think YOU could do to alleviate some of these frustrations/stresses/conflict issues?

10 What outcome would you like to see for resolving some of these situations?

SETTING TARGETS

Remember that targets need to be fully agreed and understood by the appraisee if you want them to achieve their best.

Ten questions

1 What personal objectives or targets would you like to set yourself for the year ahead?

2 How specific can you be about those targets?

3 What time are you allocating to them?

4 Are they achievable?

5 How will we check that these have been attained?

6 I would like to suggest a further target for you, which is

_____

7 How do you feel about that target?

8 What can I do to help you achieve your target?

9 What do you think your colleagues can do to help you achieve your target?

10 What can you do to achieve your target?

THE END OF THE INTERVIEW

At this stage you are drawing to a close and zipping-up the interview. This is an opportunity to receive feedback, since it is important to ask about your own performance. There are many ways to achieve a result: here are a few ideas:

Ten questions

1 How do you see your future career or job?

2 Is there anything you would like to ask me?

3 How do you see me?

4 In what ways can I help and support you?

5 Are there any specific ways in which I could improve your working life?

6 How do you think we might best develop your skills, knowledge or interest?

7 Are there any other areas that we need to discuss?

8 How do you feel this session has gone?

9 How are you now feeling about . . . ?

10 When would you like us to meet again to discuss . . . ?

■ HINTS ON HOW TO SET TARGETS

Having thought about possible questions at different stages of the interview, I now want to emphasize the importance of target-setting. Who sets the targets? The *interviewee*. Yes, the interviewee, because if you impose your targets without any consultation, then, human nature being what it is, you will meet with resistance. It is better to ask first what is their opinion about a realistic target. Then you can add your thoughts on the subject. For example, 'What targets would you like to set yourself for next year?' Remember to go for small successes: many members of staff set unachievable targets because they want to please you. Give them permission to lower their sights in order to enjoy a sense of achievement.

Now think CATS:

C	Checkable
A	Achievable
T	Timed
S	Specific

A target needs to be *checkable* to ascertain if it has been met. In order to be able to check a target you will need to ensure that the following criteria have been met.

It must be *achievable*. Some staff give themselves unachievable targets such as 'always to feel happy at work' or 'to achieve the best results in the organization, above everyone else' which is also likely to be unachievable.

Targets need to have a time element, otherwise, by the next appraisal it could mean nothing has happened. So what

first time MANAGER

you need to hear is, 'I want to clear project B in three months' time'.

Also, targets must be *specific*. If someone says to you that one of their targets is to 'be professional in their job' you will need to ask them how they intend to be more professional or, 'what would you be doing differently in order to become more professional in your job?'

Then add your targets, following the same guidelines. Always check that the targets have been understood and also what is expected from the member of staff. Ask them to repeat what you have both agreed are to be their targets.

Many misconceptions can arise at appraisals. Two people can give totally different accounts of the same proceedings, so summarize and check at the end of the meeting what you have both agreed and write it down in a formal way. Many companies have special forms to ensure uniformity.

■ RECORDING TARGETS

When the targets have been agreed, it is important to make a note of them. Keep in mind the elements of target-setting and create some kind of record-keeping that incorporates the following. These are only guidelines and can be adapted according to your work setting and desired outcomes:

Action plan

This will need to be completed by appraiser and appraisee. Set down each target and then complete the assembled columns for:

TABLE 4

TARGET	SUPPORT REQUIRED		TARGET		
	Resources	Training	Timeline (by when)	Strategies (how)	Criteria for monitoring attainment
1					
2					
3					
4					

■ Checklist for appraisal

1 Before the interview arrange a pre-meeting to establish desired ends.

2 Decide on a suitable time and place.

3 Request any relevant material.

4 Collect, assemble and read any written information.

5 If necessary, or if required, select key areas of mutual, individual or organizational issues for discussion.

6 Allocate time. Approximately one-and-a-half hours would appear to be the best timespan on any one occasion in order to focus upon an appraisee. Longer than this and the interview becomes a chat.

7 Choose an appropriate setting for the interview to take place.

8 If necessary, book the room. Redirect all telephone calls. Ensure the room is comfortable, the seats are of the same height and facing each other.

9 Put a DO NOT DISTURB sign to avoid interruptions.

10 In order to get the best out of the interview, discuss desired outcomes, for both you and the appraisee.

During the interview

1   Establish contact and rapport.

2   Create a positive relationship and climate.

3   Listen actively. The appraiser should only talk 10–20 per cent of the time, the appraisee 80–90 per cent of the time.

4   Ask open questions. Ask 'How?' and 'What?' not 'Why?'.

5   Check what you think you are saying and what you are hearing or agreeing.

6   Summarize periodically.

7   Address difficult situations rather than avoid them.

8   Reflect upon what has been decided.

9   Be assertive, not aggressive or passive.

10 Give information and/or support.

■ Resolving issues and concerns

1   Try to solve the issues and concerns raised by the appraisee.

2   Handle issues, concerns or difficulties caused by yourself.

3   Negotiate for some agreement on a win-win basis so that you both feel positive; this is different from compromise.

4   Do address any conflicting issues or any conflicting areas which have come to light.

5   Clarify the appraisee's needs, wants and expectations.

6   Recognize differing values between you and the appraisee and avoid entrenched attitudes.

7   Empathize with the appraisee's workload, role and aspirations.

8   Be able to act skilfully across a wide repertoire of behaviours and relationships.

9   Stay with the emotions that might be expressed.

10 Give feedback and ask for feedback. Let the appraisee know how they are doing and ask them how you are doing.

■ After the interview

1 Write down clearly the agreed outcome.

2 Send a copy to the appraisee.

3 Check with the appraisee that this is what was agreed.

4 Ask them to sign the document and return it to you.

5 Take appropriate action to meet any agreed outcomes.

6 Check periodically the progress of the appraisee and set out their agreed targets.

7 From time to time check that these targets are being attained as you monitor them.

8 Leave any interview notes and points arising from the interview confidential, or as agreed with the appraisee for their access.

9 Support the appraisee and either initiate or check with them any staff development needs which may have arisen from the appraisal interview.

10 As a manager, make sure you establish what motivates the appraisee and then use their strengths in the future.

■ THE A–Z OF GETTING THE BEST OUT OF YOUR STAFF

Remember

A	Appraise them
B	Believe in them
C	Communicate freely
D	Disagree without being disagreeable
E	Encourage staff development
F	Feedback helps improve performance
G	Show genuine feelings
H	Humour helps harmony
I	Ideas are good
J	Join in and participate
K	Kill rumours
L	Like and respect them
M	Motivate them
N	Nurture them
O	Openly and honestly interact
P	Praise, praise, praise!
Q	Quiet words help in good relationships
R	Reward enthusiasm
S	Socialize occasionally
T	Trust them
U	Understand their points of view
V	Value them
W	Win-win is what to aim for
X	Extra effort brings dividends
Y	Youth is good, experience great
Z	Zeal brings its own rewards

CONCLUSION

I hope that this book has helped you to recognize that you already have many skills you can be proud of, but that there may be skills that you need to develop, such as working towards being a better listener. Now you are fully aware of the multiplicity of skills needed when carrying out an inter view, you can begin to learn them.

You should now be conscious of how your body language can portray your thoughts or feelings or, just as important, how people can misread your motives because of your body language. When you are anxious in dealing with some staff, hopefully you now remember to hold your body in a confident manner until you start to feel more positive.

When you interview people, you will probably remember how the setting can affect the interview. Not only seating arrangements, but noise, adornments and smells can all have a subtle affect upon the whole procedure.

Remember to reframe negative statements when talking with your staff. Try not to make too many assumptions about people. Ask them what they think, give and ask for honest feedback. Ensure that your appraisals are done in a belief that they are to support your staff's development. That appraisals are a two-way process in which you as a manager will gain feedback and discover how to assist your staff.

You really have to work hard at motivating your staff, although according to one theory it is possible to over-stimulate.

Others believe that it is impossible to motivate staff and that they must do it for themselves. Remember that members of your staff will be driven by different incentives, and some may need to be empowered, given extra responsibility, status, titles, or a different job. However they differ, virtually all of them will be motivated by praise and will give of their best when the right relationships are in place.

Notes

■ Notes